IBURG AUDIO+SCORE

C000156024

Ludwig van Beethoven

Concerto No. 3 for Piano and Orchestra
in C minor / c-Moll
Op. 37

Edited by / Herausgegeben von
Richard Clarke

EULENBURG

EAS 127
ISBN 978-3-7957-6527-9
ISMN M-2002-2350-7

© 2007 Ernst Eulenburg & Co GmbH, Mainz
for Europe excluding the British Isles
Ernst Eulenburg Ltd, London
for all other countries
Edition based on Eulenburg Study Score ETP 704
CD ℗ & © 1988 Naxos Rights International Ltd

Ernst Eulenburg Ltd
48 Great Marlborough Street
London W1F 7BB

Contents / Inhalt

Preface

Composed: 1800, Vienna
First performance: 5 April 1803, Theater an der Wien;
Ludwig van Beethoven, piano
Original publisher: Kunst- und Industriekontor, Vienna, 1804 (parts only);
full score, Ph. Fr. Dunst, 1834
Instrumentation: 2 Flutes, 2 Oboes, 2 Clarinets, 2 Bassoons –
2 Horns, 2 Trumpets – Timpani – Strings
Duration: ca. 35 minutes

Seven concertos by Beethoven appeared in print in the composer's lifetime: five for piano, one for violin, plus the 'Triple Concerto' for violin, cello and piano. In addition he is believed to have completed three earlier ones – for piano, violin and oboe respectively – which are either wholly or partly lost. There are also substantial sketches for another Triple Concerto and a Sixth Piano Concerto. However only one of these works is in a minor key: the Third Piano Concerto, composed during 1800–3. It is, moreover, in C minor, often described as Beethoven's 'heroic' or 'Promethean' key. That Beethoven had a marked predilection for C minor is clear enough if one looks at a list of the works he produced in the decade leading up this concerto: there are two piano sonatas in C minor (Op. 10, No. 1, and Op. 13, the *Pathétique*), a string quartet (Op. 18, No. 4), a piano trio (Op. 1, No. 3) and a string trio (Op. 9, No. 3).

The Third Piano Concerto, however, was Beethoven's first orchestral work in C minor, and that in itself can be taken as a sign of the importance he attached to it. When he began working on the concerto Beethoven probably hoped to be able to play it at his benefit concert on 2 April 1800 in Vienna – the concert which saw the premiere of his recently-completed Symphony No. 1 – but it appears not to have been finished in time. Beethoven continued to work on the concerto for another two years: the first performance took place on 5 April 1803, with Beethoven himself as soloist. In fact he was evidently planning the concerto in his mind some time before 1800. An entry in his sketchbook, made during his journey to Berlin in 1796, reads 'To the Concerto in C minor kettledrum in the cadenza' – an idea which eventually came to fruition in the hushed piano-timpani exchanges after the concerto's first movement solo cadenza (I: bars 481–8).

So, all in all, work on the Third Piano Concerto appears to have occupied Beethoven, consciously or unconsciously, for at least seven years. Given the grandeur and originality of the work's conception, plus the fact that this was to be the first big public demonstration of his 'C minor mode', it is not surprising that he should have taken such pains to get it right.

Almost certainly, though, there was another factor weighing on Beethoven's mind. When the 22-year-old Beethoven set off for Vienna from his native Bonn in 1792, his patron Count Waldstein made the following entry in Beethoven's personal album:

'Dear Beethoven. You are going to Vienna in fulfilment of your long-frustrated wishes. The Genius of Mozart is still mourning and weeping the death of her pupil. [Mozart had died in December 1791.] She has found a refuge but no occupation with the inexhaustible Haydn; through him she wishes to form a union with another. With the help of assiduous labour you shall receive the spirit of Mozart from Haydn's hands.'

One work of Mozart that had made a particularly powerful impression on the young Beethoven was the Piano Concerto No. 24 in C minor, K491. The composer J. B. Cramer recalled Beethoven's excitement after a performance of the Mozart concerto at the Augarten, Vienna, in 1799, the year before he began work on his own C minor Concerto: 'Cramer, Cramer! We shall never be able to do anything like that!' According to Cramer, Beethoven singled out the sighing chromatic phrase in the 6/8 coda of Mozart's finale (K491, III: bars 241–2ff.), a striking echo of which can be heard in the finale of his own *Appassionata* Sonata (Op. 57, III: bars 86–89). The opening theme of Mozart's concerto also casts an unmistakable shadow over the opening of Beethoven's Piano Trio Op. 1 No. 3, composed in 1794–5, so the Augarten concert clearly was not Beethoven's first encounter with Mozart's masterpiece. Yet the debt to Mozart's K491 is if anything still more obvious in the first movement of Beethoven's Third Piano Concerto. Like Mozart's K491, Beethoven's concerto begins with a theme in octaves, *piano* (strings alone in Beethoven, strings plus bassoons in Mozart); moreover the first two pitches – C and E flat – are identical. Then in the remarkable piano-timpani exchanges noted above, the soloist's rippling semiquaver figures recall the similar piano figurations (punctuated by *piano* trumpets and timpani) in the coda of Mozart's opening movement.

In such passages it is hard to resist the impression that Beethoven is fully conscious of himself as the inheritor of 'the spirit of Mozart', and presumably of the responsibility that entailed. However Beethoven is never guilty of mere imitation in his own C minor Concerto, and in more general structural terms the Third Piano Concerto follows a very different course from any of Mozart's concertos. One major difference in approach can be found in the first movement's orchestral exposition, before the piano's arresting first solo entry in bar 111. In his later piano concertos Mozart's orchestral expositions present some, or all, of the first major themes, all more or less securely in the home key. Beethoven's orchestral introduction in Op. 37 is not only of substantial length (110 bars), but also contains two dramatic modulations. The appearance of the second main theme in E flat major (bar 50ff.) is preceded by a long preparation on the dominant of E flat *minor* (bars 36–48), thus reinforcing the move towards the new key. It is only at bar 61 that the harmony swerves magically back to C – only now it is C *major*, the move underlined by trumpets and drums. The mode remains uncertain – veering between the tonic major and minor – until bar 85.

Beethoven had already included arresting feints towards new keys in the orchestral introductions of his first and second piano concertos, but here the move is more emphatic – more in keeping with the kind of dramatized modulation one encounters in his symphonic first movements. It has been argued by some, most famously by Tovey in his *Essays in Musical Analysis*, that this was a mistake on Beethoven's part: 'This is sheer symphonic exposition; it rouses no expectation of the entry of a solo instrument, and [...] leaves nothing essential for the piano when its time comes'. In other words, in a true concerto it is up to the soloist to inaugurate dramatic tonal moves; having the orchestra do so before the pianist enters is stealing too much of his thunder.

This however begs the question why Beethoven's Third Piano Concerto has continued to be so popular with soloists and audiences alike, not to mention why a composer like Brahms – one of the most thoughtful of 19th-century composers when it came to matters of structure – should have been inspired to imitate this 'symphonic' attitude to tonality in the orchestral exposition of his own First Piano Concerto in D minor (1854-8). It is true that Beethoven never repeated this experiment in any of his later concertos, but that is not in itself evidence that he reached the same conclusion as Tovey. In any case, Beethoven does leave plenty for the soloist to do in dramatic-architectural terms. Another striking feature of the Third Piano Concerto's opening orchestral exposition is Beethoven's use of silence, notably in bars 1–23. Whatever Tovey may allege, this does create an air of expectancy, only partly allayed by the more continuous nature of the rest of the exposition, and it is further reinforced by the use of rests at the end of the concluding orchestral tutti (bars 109–110). The piano's powerful first entry is similarly punctuated by rests, while the subsequent three-octave unison restatement of the concerto's first theme suggests that the soloist is attempting to present himself as an equal contender to the orchestra. But the piano's version of the theme's second phrase (bars 118–121) is melodically embellished, and leads smoothly into the next phrase, also elegantly decorated. In the expanded version of the exposition that follows, the soloist can be seen as striving to bring a lyrical continuity to ideas which previously were tersely discrete.

Another 'essential' function left to the soloist in the first movement of the Third Piano Concerto is one that might be called 'formal punctuation'. The stirring rising scales of the piano's first entry return at two key points in the structure: they herald the beginning of the development section at bars 249–252, again after a long orchestral tutti, and, unbroken by rests this time, they bring about the final reinforcement of the tonic (bars 503–5). Significantly, they do not appear in the solo cadenza, however suitable they may be for virtuoso development at this point. Incidentally, the piano's modulations in the first phase of the cadenza (bars 417–433) take it much further from the tonic C minor than at any stage in the opening orchestral exposition.

Still more unusual tonal adventures are initiated by the soloist later in the concerto. It is the piano, unaccompanied, which begins the *Largo* slow movement in the key of E major – a tonality so remote from C minor that it can still create an effect of surprise even today. This time Beethoven may have had a Haydn model in mind: Haydn's String Quartet Op. 74 No. 3 in G minor also has a *Largo* slow movement in E major, producing a similarly startling effect in context. Mozart generally avoided such extreme tonal contrasts between movements in his orchestral and chamber works. But Beethoven's intensely expressive recollection of the first movement's C tonality at the climax of the *Largo*'s opening melody (bar 11) – with a dislocating melodic leap of a tenth in the right hand and quasi-tremolando tenths in the left – is an entirely personal stroke. So too is the piano's 'reinterpretation' of its repeated A flats as G sharps at bar 261 of the finale, leading to a dreamlike recollection of the slow movement's E major, the romantic fantastical effect underlined by the marking *con Ped*. It is also the piano, again unaccompanied, which achieves the concerto's final clinching move from tragic C minor to joyous, even comedic C major at the beginning of the *Presto* coda, in the process turning the finale's opening G-A flat quavers to a brighter, major-inflected G sharp-A – this after a spectacular protracted solo arabesque which takes in almost the entire range of the piano as Beethoven knew it in 1803.

Other examples of Beethoven's imaginative daring in his piano writing can be found on page after page of this score. Note, for example, the exquisite flowing first inversion triads in bars 156–9 of the first movement: the *legato* three-octave semiquavers passed between the hands in the development (I: bars 295–306); or the liquid multiple trills, with imitations based on the first theme in both hands, at the end of the cadenza (I: bar 470–6) – an effect that looks forward to the quietly ecstatic closing moments of Beethoven's last piano sonata, Op. 111, and poses a greater technical challenge for the soloist than any of the cascading arpeggios in the cadenza's first section. In such passages, Beethoven steps into territory barely visited in the piano works of Mozart and Haydn. Just as remarkable, in a different kind of way, is the cadenza of the *Largo*: a single unaccompanied line for the right hand, florid at first, but grow-ing increasingly vocal in style, and marked *sempre con gran espressione* ('always with great expression') – an effect like that later achieved by Schumann in the piano recitative of his 'Der Dichter spricht' ('The Poet Speaks') from *Kinderszenen*. In such passages it is Beethoven the fully-fledged romantic virtuoso-poet, rather than the inheritor of the 'spirit of Mozart', who stands centre-stage.

Stephen Johnson

Vorwort

komponiert: 1800 in Wien
Uraufführung: 5. April 1803 im Theater an der Wien
mit Beethoven am Klavier
Originalverlag: Kunst- und Industriekontor, Wien, 1804 (nur Stimmen);
Partiturausgabe: Ph. Fr. Dunst, 1834
Orchesterbesetzung: 2 Flöten, 2 Oboen, 2 Klarinetten, 2 Fagotte –
2 Hörner, 2 Trompeten – Pauken – Streicher
Spieldauer: etwa 35 Minuten

Sieben Konzerte Beethovens erschienen zu Lebzeiten des Komponisten im Druck: fünf für Klavier, eines für Violine und das Tripelkonzert für Violine, Cello und Klavier op. 56. Außerdem nimmt man an, dass er drei frühere vollendet habe – für Klavier, Violine bzw. für Oboe –, die entweder zur Gänze oder teilweise verloren gegangen sind. Hinzu kommen umfangreiche Skizzen zu einem weiteren Tripelkonzert und einem sechsten Klavierkonzert. Nur eins dieser Werke jedoch steht in einer Moll-Tonart: das 3. Klavierkonzert, komponiert zwischen 1800 und 1803. Darüber hinaus steht es in c-Moll, das oft als Beethovens „heroische" oder „prometheische" Tonart bezeichnet wurde. Dass Beethoven eine dezidierte Vorliebe für c-Moll hatte, geht deutlich genug aus einer Aufzählung der Werke hervor, die er in dem Jahrzehnt schuf, das diesem Konzert vorausging: zwei Klaviersonaten in c-Moll (op. 10,1 und op. 13, die *Pathétique*), ein Streichquartett (op. 18,4), ein Klaviertrio (op. 1,3) und ein Streichtrio (op. 9,3).

Das dritte Klavierkonzert indes war Beethovens erstes Orchesterwerk in c-Moll, und dies kann an sich selber schon als Zeichen für die Bedeutung angesehen werden, die er ihm beimaß. Als Beethoven mit der Arbeit am Werk begann, hoffte er wahrscheinlich, es in seinem Wiener Benefizkonzert am 2. April 1800 zu spielen – jenem Konzert, das die Uraufführung seiner unlängst vollendeten 1. Sinfonie sah –, doch scheint es nicht rechtzeitig fertig geworden zu sein. Beethoven setzte die Arbeit am Konzert für weitere zwei Jahre fort; die Uraufführung, mit dem Komponisten als Solist, fand am 5. April 1803 statt. Tatsächlich hatte er das Konzert offenkundig schon einige Zeit vor 1800 im Geist entworfen. Ein Eintrag in seinem Skizzenbuch aus der Zeit seiner Reise nach Berlin 1796 sieht „für das Konzert in c-moll Kesselpauke in der Kadenz" vor: ein Einfall, der schließlich im gedämpften Wechselspiel zwischen Piano und Timpani nach der Solokadenz des ersten Satzes zur Reife gelangte (1. Satz, Takt 481–488).

Mithin scheint Beethoven alles in allem die Arbeit am 3. Klavierkonzert, bewusst oder unbewusst, mindestens sieben Jahre lang beschäftigt zu haben. Berücksichtigt man die Großartigkeit und Originalität der Werkkonzeption, dazu die Tatsache, dass dies die erste öffentliche Demonstration seines „c-Moll-Gestus" sein sollte, überrascht es nicht, dass dem Komponisten die Ausarbeitung nicht eben leicht von der Hand ging. Mit an Sicherheit grenzender Wahrscheinlichkeit indes lag ihm ein weiterer Faktor auf der Seele. Als der 22-jährige Beethoven aus seiner Geburtsstadt Bonn 1792 nach Wien aufgebrochen war, hatte ihm sein Gönner Graf Waldstein ins Stammbuch geschrieben:

„Lieber Beethoven! Sie reisen itzt nach Wien zur Erfüllung ihrer so lange bestrittenen Wünsche. Mozarts Genius trauert noch und beweinet den Tod seines Zöglinges. [Mozart war im Dezember 1791 gestorben.] Bei dem unerschöpflichen Haydn fand er Zuflucht, aber keine Beschäftigung; durch ihn wünscht er noch einmal mit jemanden [sic] vereinigt zu werden. Durch ununterbrochenen Fleiß erhalten Sie: Mozarts Geist aus Haydns Händen."

Ein Werk Mozarts, das einen besonders nachhaltigen Eindruck auf den jungen Beethoven gemacht hatte, war das Klavierkonzert c-Moll KV 491. Der Komponist J. B. Cramer erinnerte daran, wie ergriffen Beethoven 1799, im Jahr vor Beginn der Arbeit an seinem eigenen c-Moll-Konzert, nach einer Aufführung des Mozart-Konzerts im Wiener Augarten war: „Cramer, Cramer! Wir werden niemals im Stande sein, etwas Ähnliches zu machen!" Nach Cramer hatte es Beethoven vor allem die seufzende chromatische Phrase in der 6/8-Coda von Mozarts Finale angetan (KV 491, 3. Satz, T. 242-242ff.); ein frappanter Nachhall dieser Passage lässt sich im Finale seiner eigenen *Appassionata*-Sonate vernehmen (op. 57, 3. Satz, T. 86-89). Das Anfangsthema von Mozarts Konzert wirft auch einen unmissverständlichen Schatten über den Beginn des Beethovenschen Klaviertrios op. 1,3, komponiert 1794 bis 1795, woraus erhellt, dass das Konzert im Augarten nicht Beethovens erste Begegnung mit Mozarts Meisterwerk war. Doch nirgendwo schuldet Beethoven dem KV 491 Mozarts so viel wie im ersten Satz seines 3. Klavierkonzerts. Wie bei Mozart beginnt Beethovens Konzert *piano* und oktaviert (bei Beethoven Streicher allein – bei Mozart Streicher + Fagotte); darüber hinaus sind die ersten beiden Noten (C und Es) identisch. Sodann erinnern in dem eingangs erwähnten bemerkenswerten Piano-Timpani-Dialog die gekräuselten Sechzehntelfiguren des Solisten an ähnliche Klavierfigurationen (zum punktierten Rhythmus, *piano*, von Trompeten und Pauken) in der Coda von Mozarts Eröffnungssatz.

In solchen Passagen lässt sich kaum dem Eindruck widerstehen, dass Beethoven sich seiner selbst als des Erben von „Mozarts Geist" (und mutmaßlich der Verantwortung, die solche Erbschaft mit sich bringt) voll bewusst ist. Der bloßen Nachahmung freilich macht sich Beethoven in seinem c-Moll-Konzert nie schuldig und in allgemeiner struktureller Hinsicht schlägt das 3. Klavierkonzert eine ganz andere Richtung ein als irgendeines der Mozart-Konzerte. Ein größerer Unterschied in der Herangehensweise z.B. findet sich in der Orchester-Einleitung des ersten Satzes vor dem ersten zupackenden Solo-Einsatz des Klaviers in Takt 111. In seinen späten Klavierkonzerten stellen Mozarts Orchester-Einleitungen einige oder alle ersten Hauptthemen vor, alle mehr oder weniger stabil in ihrer Grundtonart. Beethovens Orchester-Einleitung im Opus 37 ist nicht nur von erheblicher Länge (110 Takte), sondern enthält auch zwei dramatische Modulationen. Dem Auftritt des zweiten Hauptthemas in Es-

Dur (T. 50ff.) geht eine lange Vorbereitung auf der Dominante von es-*Moll* voraus (T. 36–48), die die Tendenz zur neuen Tonart bekräftigt. Erst in Takt 61 weicht die Harmonie magisch zurück nach C – nur, dass es sich jetzt um C-*Dur* handelt, wobei dieser Schritt noch von Trompeten und Pauken akzentuiert wird. Bis Takt 85 bleibt das Tongeschlecht – indem es zwischen Tonika-Dur und -Moll wechselt – unbestimmt.

Schon in die Orchester-Einleitungen seines ersten und zweiten Klavierkonzerts hatte Beethoven frappierende Modulationsstrategien eingefügt, doch hier ist der Richtungswechsel noch emphatischer – noch mehr auf der Höhe jener dramatisierten Modulationsverläufe, denen man in den Anfangssätzen seiner Sinfonien begegnet. Es ist von einigen eingewendet worden, am berühmtesten von Tovey in seinen *Essays in Musical Analysis,* dass dies seitens Beethovens ein Fehler gewesen sei: „Dies ist eine rein sinfonische Exposition; sie weckt keine Neugier auf den Eintritt eines Soloinstruments, und […] lässt dem Klavier nichts Wesentliches mehr zu sagen, wenn seine Zeit gekommen ist.“ Mit anderen Worten: In einem echten Konzert ist es Aufgabe des Solisten, dramatische Tonartwechsel zu stiften; lässt man dies das Orchester tun, bevor der Pianist einsetzt, nimmt man diesem zu viel von seinem Aplomb.

Das wirft allerdings die Frage auf, warum Beethovens 3. Klavierkonzert sich bis heute bei Solisten und beim Publikum solcher Beliebtheit erfreut; von der Frage ganz zu schweigen, warum ein Komponist wie Brahms – im Hinblick auf Struktur einer der gedankenreichsten Komponisten des 19. Jahrhunderts – es sich angelegen sein ließ, diese „sinfonische“ Haltung gegenüber Tonartlichkeit in der Orchestereinleitung seines eigenen 1. Klavierkonzerts in d-Moll (1854–1858) nachzuahmen. Wahr ist, dass Beethoven dieses Experiment in keinem seiner späteren Konzerte mehr wiederholte, aber das ist noch kein Beleg dafür, dass er zu derselben Schlussfolgerung gelangte wie Tovey. Auf alle Fälle lässt Beethoven dem Solisten in dramatisch-architektonischer Hinsicht viel zu tun übrig. Ein weiterer auffälliger Zug in der Orchester-Einleitung des dritten Klavierkonzerts ist Beethovens Verwendung von Pausen, etwa in den Takten 1–23. Was immer Tovey behaupten mag – dies beschwört tatsächlich eine Atmosphäre gespannter Erwartung herauf, die nur teilweise vom weniger diskontinuierlichen Verlauf der restlichen Exposition besänftigt und später neu bekräftigt wird durch den Einsatz von Pausen nach dem abschließenden Orchester-Tutti in Takt 109–110. Auf ähnliche Weise wird der kraftvolle erste Eintritt des Klaviers von Pausen interpunktiert, während die folgende Wiederbestätigung des ersten Themas im Drei-Oktaven-Unisono den Eindruck erweckt, als wolle sich der Solist dem Orchester als gleichberechtigter Mitstreiter präsentieren. Die Version des Themen-Nachsatzes im Klavier (T. 118–121) ist jedoch melodisch ausgeziert und geleitet ebenmäßig zur nächsten, ebenfalls elegant umspielten Periode. Aus der erweiterten Version der Exposition, die darauf folgt, lässt sich ersehen, wie dem Solisten daran gelegen ist, jenen Ideen, die zuvor konzis für sich allein standen, lyrische Kontinuität zu verleihen.

Eine weitere „wesentliche“ Funktion, die im ersten Satz des 3. Klavierkonzerts dem Solisten zufällt, könnte man „formale Interpunktion“ nennen. Die agitatorisch aufschnellenden Skalen beim ersten Einsatz des Klaviers kehren an zwei formalen Schlüsselstellen wieder: Sie verkünden, wiederum nach einem langen Orchester-Tutti, den Beginn der Durchführung (T. 249–252); und sie stellen, diesmal nicht von Pausen unterbrochen, die finale Wiederbekräftigung der Tonika her (T. 503–505). Bezeichnenderweise erscheinen sie nicht in der Solokadenz, wie geeignet sie an dieser Stelle für virtuose Verarbeitung auch wären. Im übrigen entfernen sich die Modulationen des Klaviers im ersten Abschnitt der Kadenz (T. 417–433) viel weiter vom tonikalen c-Moll als in irgendeiner Phase der einleitenden Orchester-Exposition.

Noch ungewöhnlichere Tonarten-Abenteuer werden vom Solisten im späteren Verlauf des Konzerts gewagt. Es ist das Klavier, das – unbegleitet – den langsamen Satz (*Largo*) in der Tonart E-Dur beginnt, einer Tonstufe, so weit entfernt von c-Moll, dass sie selbst heute noch einen Überraschungseffekt auslösen kann. Diesmal mochte Beethoven ein Modell von Haydn im Sinn gehabt haben: Haydns Streichquartett op. 74,3 in g-Moll hat ebenfalls als langsamen Satz ein *Largo* in E-Dur, das im Kontext der übrigen Sätze eine ähnlich frappante Wirkung erzielt. Mozart vermied im Allgemeinen solche extremen tonartlichen Kontraste zwischen den Sätzen seiner Orchester- oder Kammermusik. Doch Beethovens hochexpressive Erinnerung der C-Tonalität des ersten Satzes auf dem Höhepunkt der Eröffnungsmelodie des *Largo* (Takt 11) – mit einem dislozierenden melodischen Dezimensprung in der rechten Hand und Quasi-tremolando-Dezimen in der Linken – folgt einem ganz und gar persönlichen Stil. Dies gilt auch für die „Rückdeutung" der repetierten Noten As zu Gis im Klavier in Takt 261 des Schlusssatzes, die zu einer traumgleichen Rückerinnerung des E-Dur aus dem langsamen Satz führt, wobei der romantisch-phantastische Effekt noch unterstrichen wird von der Anweisung *con Ped.* Es ist auch das – wiederum unbegleitete – Klavier, das den letzten entscheidenden Schritt des Konzerts von tragischem c-Moll zu freudevollem, sogar komödiantischem C-Dur zu Beginn der *Presto*-Coda gewinnt und in diesem Verlauf die G-As-Achtel, die den Finalsatz eröffnen, in ein helleres, nach Dur geneigtes Gis-A wandeln – dies nach einer spektakulär verlängerten Solo-Arabeske, die beinahe den ganzen Ambitus der Klaviatur umgreift, wie sie Beethoven 1803 zur Verfügung stand.

Andere Beispiele für die imaginative Kühnheit von Beethovens Klaviersatz lassen sich in dieser Partitur Seite für Seite finden. Man beachte zum Beispiel die exquisit fließenden Dreiklänge in der ersten Umkehrung in Takt 156–159 des ersten Satzes; die legato-Sechzehntel in der Durchführung (1. Satz, T. 295–306), die über drei Oktaven von Hand zu Hand wechseln; oder die Trillerketten mit den Imitationen auf der Grundlage des ersten Themas in beiden Händen am Ende der Kadenz (1. Satz, T. 470–476): ein Effekt, der bereits vorausblickt auf den ruhig-ekstatischen Schluss der letzten Variation im 2. Satz von Beethovens letzter Klaviersonate op. 111 und den Solisten vor größere technische Herausforderungen stellt als eine der Arpeggio-Kaskaden im ersten Abschnitt der Kadenz. In solchen Passagen beschreitet Beethoven eine Region, die in den Klavierwerken von Mozart und Haydn noch kaum betreten wurde. Auf andere Weise ebenso bemerkenswert ist die Kadenz des Largo: eine einzige unbegleitete Linie für die rechte Hand, zunächst ornamental, dann im Stil immer gesanglicher werdend und mit *sempre con gran espressione* bezeichnet („ständig mit großer Empfindung") – ein Effekt ähnlich dem, den Schumann später im Klavier-Rezitativ seines „Der Dichter spricht" aus den *Kinderszenen* op. 15 erzielte. In solchen Passagen ist es Beethoven eher als voll entwickelter romantischer Virtuose und Tondichter denn als Erbe von „Mozarts Geist", der im Rampenlicht steht.

Stephen Johnson
Übersetzung: Wolfgang Schlüter

Dem Prinzen Louis Ferdinand von Preußen gewidmet

Piano Concerto No. 3

Ludwig van Beethoven
(1770–1827)
Op. 37

I. Allegro con brio

EAS 127

© 2007 Ernst Eulenburg Ltd, London
and Ernst Eulenburg & Co GmbH, Mainz

4

18

EAS 127

24

II. **Largo**

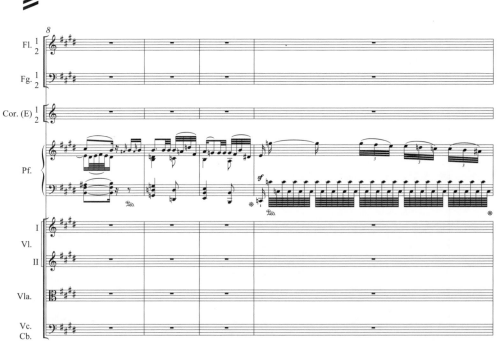

40

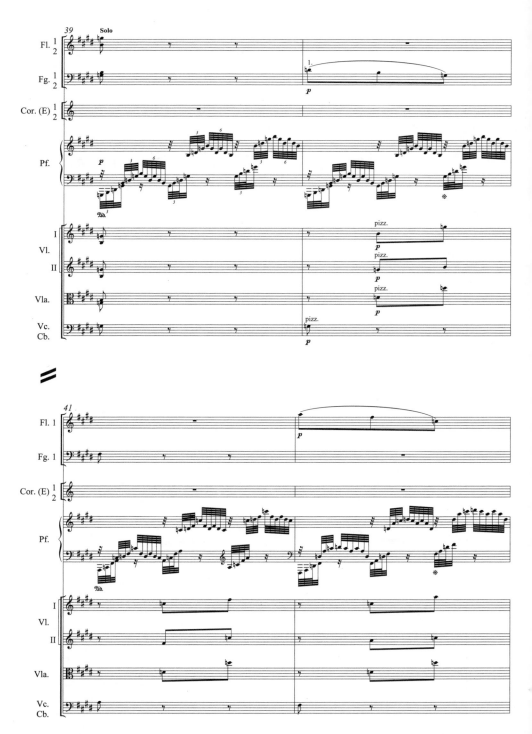

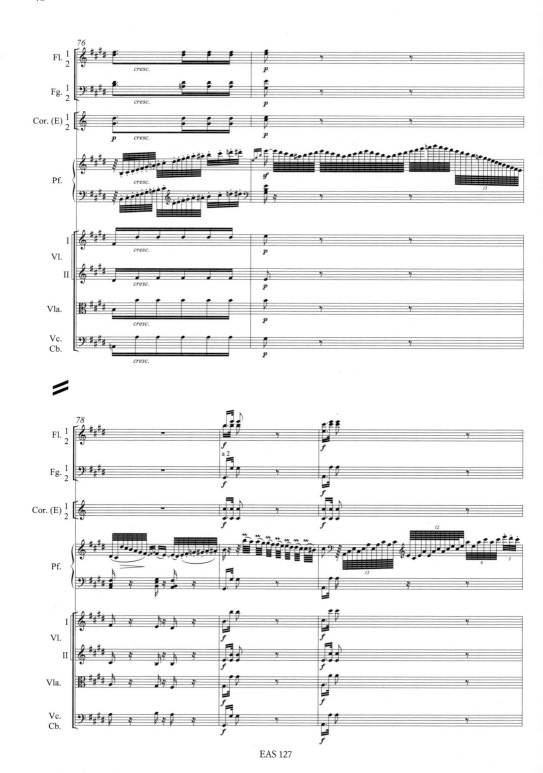

III. **Rondo**
Allegro

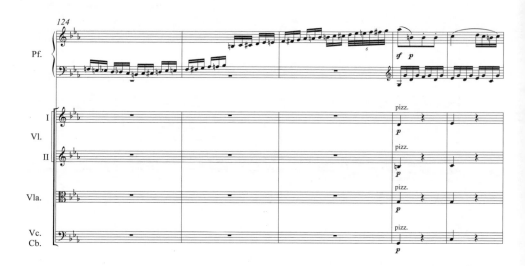

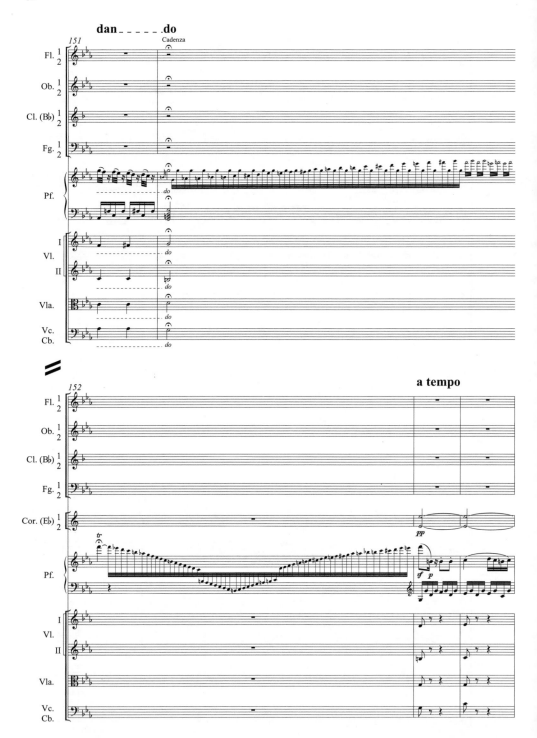

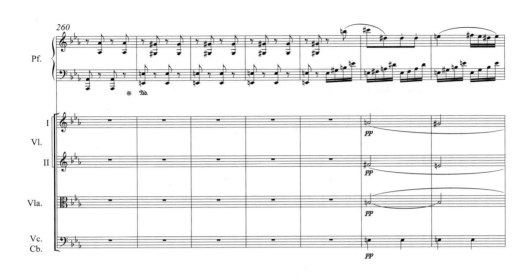

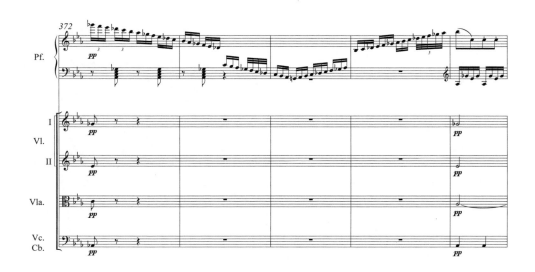

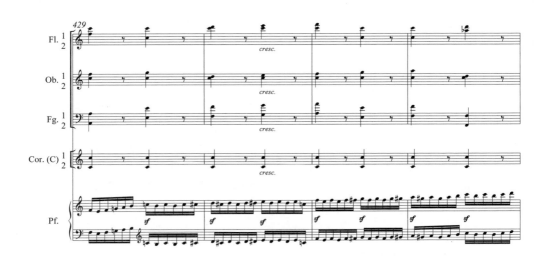

THE ART OF SCORE-READING

The first steps

A score contains the entire musical text of a musical work in order that the conductor and everyone who wants to study the piece more thoroughly can see exactly which passages are being played by the orchestra or ensemble. The parts of the individual instruments are arranged in such a way that all notes played at the same time are written one below the other.

Scores help to listen to, understand and interpret musical works. Those who only listen to music are unaware of many important details which, after some practice, become apparent when reading the score while listening to the music. The clear structure of the score helps to easily understand the compositional style and the characteristic features of a piece – this is a prerequisite not only for any analysis but also for the musician's own performance and interpretation.

The simplest method of score-reading is to read an individual part by concentrating on an individual part that can be heard particularly well. The most suitable pieces to begin with are concertos with solo instruments such as Beethoven's Romance in F major for violin and orchestra (example 1) or orchestral songs (with them, one may easily follow the text). Furthermore, in many classical orchestral works, it is quite easy to follow the lead part of the principal violin, or the bass part in baroque compositions for orchestra.

The next step is to try to change from one part to another and vice versa and follow the part that is leading. Little by little, you learn to find distinctive parts you hear in the score as well and follow them in the corresponding staff. This can be very easily tried out with Beethoven's Symphony No. 5 (example 2). To read the score, it is also helpful to count the bars. This technique is rather useful in the case of confusing or complex scores, such as those of contemporary music, and is particularly suitable when you do not want to lag behind in any case. It should be your aim, however, to eventually give up counting the bars and to read the score by first following individual parts and then going over to section-by-section or selective reading (see next page).

Example 1 · from: Romance for violin and orchestra in F major by Beethoven

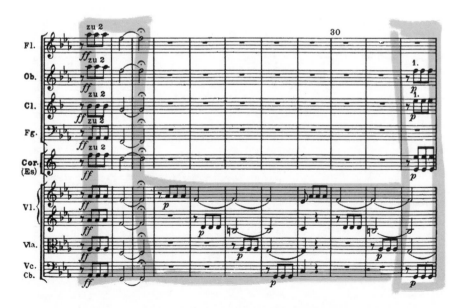

Example 2 · from: Symphony No. 5 C-minor by Beethoven

Further score-reading techniques

Example 3 · from: Symphony No. 100 G major 'Military' by Haydn

Example 4 · from: Symphony No. 41 C major 'Jupiter' by W. A. Mozart

Section-by-section reading

This technique is suitable for application in the 'Military' Symphony by Haydn (example 3). In bb. 260-264, the parts are mostly in parallel motion so that it is quite easy to take in the section as a whole. In the strings, the texture is homophonic (i.e. all instruments play the same rhythm), consisting of tone repetitions in the lower parts while there is a little more movement in the part of the first violin. At the same time, the tones of the winds are stationary (i.e. long sustained notes), serving as harmonic filling-in. If need be, they can also be read en bloc.

Such block-like structures often consist of unison figures (= all instruments play the same), such as at the beginning of Mozart's Jupiter Symphony (example 4). Here, the score-reading can first be limited to the strings section which carries the melody alone in bb. 3-4 and contains all important information.

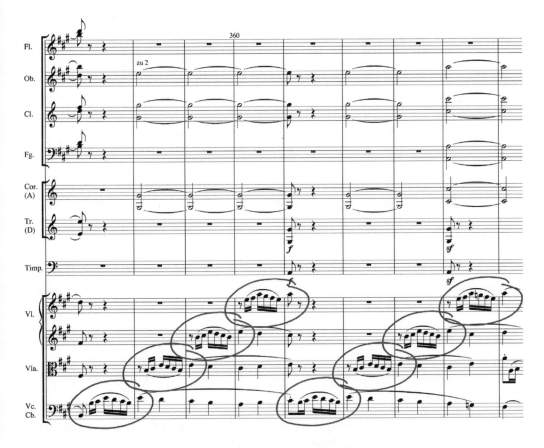

Example 5 · from: Symphony No. 7 A major by Beethoven

Selektive reading

Using this technique, you concentrate on selected parts (lead parts, conspicuous passages) in the score. In the excerpt from Beethoven's Symphony No. 7 (example 5), it is the semiquaver motif that, originating with the violoncellos and basses and pervading the string parts twice, is particularly well suited. The stationary tones of the winds, consisting only of the note E in various octave positions in bb. 358-363, form the harmonic foundation and play a subordinate role in score-reading. Though they are briefly noticed, it is the strings and especially the conspicuous semiquaver motif pervading the individual parts that are to be followed.

With both score-reading techniques which should be chosen according to the nature of the passage in question, it is not important in the beginning to be able to follow at once all tones and harmonies. What matters more is to recognize and comprehend sequences of movement. Everything else comes with experience.

Following contrapuntal parts

The present excerpt from Brahms's Requiem (example 6) is polyphonic, i.e. one has to be able to follow several equal parts either alternately (without lagging behind) or simultaneously. But by looking for parallel parts in the score, the notation which, at first glance, seems to be overcrowded soon becomes clearer. For example, Brahms allocates orchestral parts to each choral part. As a consequence, there are many parts written in the score but considerably fewer independent parts actually played. Hence, the large amount of written music can be reduced to a manageable quantity.

The flute, clarinet, first violins and soprano are in parallel motion. Furthermore, the tenor of oboe and viola is supported by a much-expanded, yet parallel part.
The violoncellos and bassoons too are in almost parallel motion.

The low winds and strings as well as the timpani played simultaneously with the polyphonic parts are fill-in parts which consist only of stationary tones (sustained notes). They do not need to be followed upon first reading of the score.

Seen as a whole, this excerpt is most suitable for focussing on the soprano voice as it is coupled with two instruments and, being the highest voice, can be heard very well. In addition, the text is an aid to orientation, making it easier to return from brief trips to other parts.

In fugal sections, score-reading will be easier if the entries of the theme in the score are first looked for and then marked.

Example 6 · from: A German Requiem by Brahms

The score at a glance

A **Bar lines** are solid vertical lines within the instrument sections.

B The **bar numbers** are an aid to orientation in the score. Sometimes capital letters, so-called rehearsal letters, are used instead of numbers.

C The system of parallel lines on and between which the notes are written is called **staff** (or stave). The instrument abbreviation in front of each line (here, Fl. is for 'flute') indicates to which instrument(s) the line(s) refer(s).

D The **barline at the left-hand end** of the staves connects all staves to form the **system**.

E In addition to the barline at the left-hand end of the staves, **angular brackets** connect the individual groups of instruments in a score (wind, brass and string instruments). Within these groups, the instruments are arranged according to their pitch, with the highest-pitched instrument mentioned first.
Today, the common order of instrumental parts in the score is as follows, from top to bottom:
· wind instruments
· brass instruments
· percussion instruments
· harp, piano, celesta
· solo instrument(s)
· solo voices
· choir
· string instruments

F When there are two systems on a page, they are separated from each other by two parallel **diagonal strokes**.

G Instruments the names of which are followed by 'in Bb' or (Bb) are **transposing instruments**. In this case, (Bb) indicates that the notated C is played as Bb, i.e. all tones are played a tone lower than notated. Most of the transposing instruments are easily recognizable in the score thanks to these additions. However, there are also transposing instruments without such indications in the score, such as:
· piccolo flute (in C / an octave higher)
· cor anglais (in F / a fifth lower)
· contrabassoon (in C / an octave lower)
· double bass (in C / an octave lower)

H The transposing brass instruments have no general signature but, if need be, accidentals preceding the respective tone.

I The viola part is notated in the **alto clef**, the parts of violoncello and bassoon sometimes in the **tenor clef**. Both clefs are easy to read when the player realizes that the clef frames the note C1:

alto clef   tenor clef   treble clef

J Any change of key or time is marked by a **double bar**. The alla-breve sign following in this example (¢), like the sign for four-four time (c), is a relic from an old notational practice and stands for two-two time.

100

Section-by-section reading:
For parts which, rhythmically, move in parallel motion.

Selective
reading:
The lead
part is
followed.

from: Symphony No. 4 Bb by Beethoven

A **Tempo indications** (sometimes in connection with metronome markings) are used by the composer to indicate how fast a piece shall be played.

B In the winds, two parts are usually brought together in one line. If they play the same note, the note head either has two stems or 'a2' written above it.

C Two-part chords in the staves of the strings are played by one player. If the parts shall be divided, **divisi** (divided) is written in the score. Then, at each desk, one player plays the upper notes and another player the lower notes.

D When an instrumental part contains a long rest, as in this flute part for example, its staff is often omitted until the next entry of the instrument, thus saving space. In addition, there are less page-turns, and the playing parts are arranged much clearer.

E In order to save space and arrange phrases or groups of notes more clearly, so-called abbreviations are used occasionally. The sign ♩ stands for ♪♪♪♪, with the minim indicating the duration of the repetitions and the stroke crossing the stem indicating the value of the notes to be repeated (1 stroke = quaver, 2 strokes = semiquaver, etc.). Cf. also the viola in b. 43 in which the repeated notes are first written out and then abbreviated.

Score-Reading with pupils and students!

Order this guideline for score-reading for your class! The leaflet 'The Art of Score-Reading' is available separately or as a set of copies and can be obtained free of charge while stock last.

Brochure 'The Art of Score-Reading'
Order No. ETP 9998-99 (free of charge)

Mozart for the classroom

A picture of life and travel
Mozart was not only one of the greatest composers, but also one of the best pianists of the 18th century. Like the virtuos of today, he spent a large part of his life on concert tours at the leading courts and great cities of his time.

This small brochure depicts a panorama of the musical life in Europe wich formed the background to Mozart's oeuvre. The picture is completed by a short biography and a little insight into his way of composing.

Brochure 'Mozart. A Picture of Life and Travel'
Order No. ETP 9991-99 (free of charge)

For further information, see at: www.eulenburg.de

Eulenburg

DIE KUNST
DES PARTITURLESENS

Der erste Einstieg

Eine Partitur enthält den gesamten Notentext eines Musikwerkes, damit der Dirigent und jeder, der sich näher mit dem Stück beschäftigen will, genau nachvollziehen kann, was das Orchester oder das Ensemble spielt. Dabei sind die Instrumente so angeordnet, dass alle Noten, die zur gleichen Zeit erklingen, genau untereinander stehen.
Partituren helfen beim Hören, Begreifen und Interpretieren von Musikliteratur. Wer nur zuhört, erkennt viele kostbare Kleinigkeiten nicht, die beim Mitlesen nach ein wenig Übung regelrecht sichtbar werden. Der Kompositionsstil und die Charakteristik eines Werkes lassen sich mit der übersichtlichen Partitur schnell begreifen – das ist nicht nur Grundvoraussetzung für jede Analyse, sondern auch für das eigene Spiel.

Die einfachste Methode beim Partiturlesen ist das Verfolgen einer Einzelstimme. Bei diesem Verfahren konzentriert man sich auf eine einzelne Stimme, die besonders gut zu hören ist. Zum Einstieg eignen sich dabei besonders gut Konzerte mit Soloinstrumenten wie die Romanze in F-Dur für Violine und Orchester von Beethoven (Beispiel 1) oder Orchesterlieder (bei letzteren kann man sich leicht am Text orientieren). Weiterhin kann man bei vielen klassischen Orchesterwerken die führende Stimme der ersten Violine gut verfolgen, sowie bei barocken Kompositionen für Orchester die Bass-Stimme.

In einem nächsten Schritt kann man versuchen, zwischen den Stimmen zu wechseln und jeweils die Stimme zu verfolgen, die gerade führend ist. Nach und nach lernt man dabei markante Stimmen, die man hört, auch in der Partitur zu finden und im entsprechenden Notensystem zu verfolgen. Besonders anschaulich kann man das mittels Beethovens 5. Symphonie erproben (Beispiel 2).
Eine weitere Hilfe beim Lesen der Partitur kann auch das Mitzählen der Takte sein. Dieses Verfahren hilft bei unübersichtlichen oder komplexen Partituren wie etwa zeitgenössischer Musik und eignet sich besonders, wenn man den Anschluss auf keinen Fall verlieren möchte. Ziel sollte es jedoch sein, das Mitzählen der Takte gänzlich zu verlassen und die Partitur zunächst anhand einzelner Stimmen und dann im Wechsel von blockweisem bzw. selektivem Lesen zu verfolgen (siehe nächste Seite).

Beispiel 1 · aus: Romanze für Violine und Orchester F-Dur von Beethoven

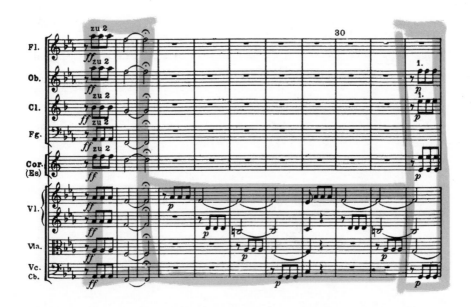

Beispiel 2 · aus: Symphonie Nr. 5 c-moll von Beethoven

Weitere Methoden des Partiturlesens

Beispiel 3 · aus: Symphonie Nr. 100 G-Dur „Militär" von Haydn

Beispiel 4 · aus: Symphonie Nr. 41 C-Dur „Jupiter" von W. A. Mozart

Blockweises Lesen

Diese Methode bietet sich in der Militär-Symphonie von Haydn an (Beispiel 3). In den T. 260-264 sind die Stimmen weitgehend parallel geführt, so dass man sie gut im Ganzen überblicken kann. In den Streichern haben wir einen homophonen Satz (d.h. alle Stimmen spielen den gleichen Rhythmus), der in den unteren Stimmen aus Tonwiederholungen besteht, während die erste Violine etwas bewegter ist. Gleichzeitig erklingen in den Bläserstimmen Liegetöne (d.h. lang ausgehaltene Töne), die als harmonischer Füllstoff dienen. Sie können bei Bedarf auch im Block gelesen werden.
Oft bestehen solche blockhaften Gebilde auch aus unisono-Figuren (= alle Stimmen spielen dasselbe), wie z.B. am Beginn der Jupiter-Symphonie von Mozart (Beispiel 4). Hier kann man sich beim Lesen zunächst nur auf den Streicherblock beschränken, der in den T. 3-4 alleine die Melodie weiterführt und bereits alle wichtigen Informationen enthält.

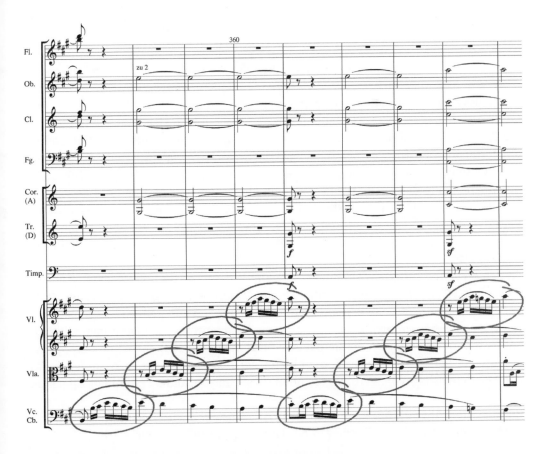

Beispiel 5 · aus: Symphonie Nr. 7 A-Dur von Beethoven

Selektives Lesen

Bei dieser Methode orientiert man sich anhand ausgewählter Stimmen (führende Stimmen, auffällige Stellen) in der Partitur. Im Ausschnitt aus Beethovens 7. Symphonie (Beispiel 5) ist hierzu das Sechzehntelmotiv geeignet, das zweimal von den Celli und Bässen ausgehend durch die Streicherstimmen wandert. Die Liegetöne der Bläser, die in den T. 358-363 sogar nur aus dem Ton e in unterschiedlichen Oktavlagen bestehen, bilden die harmonische Grundierung und spielen beim Lesen der Partitur eine untergeordnete Rolle. Man nimmt sie kurz wahr, verfolgt jedoch die Streicher und dort insbesondere das auffällige Sechzehntelmotiv in seiner Wanderung durch die einzelnen Stimmen.

Bei beiden Leseformen, zwischen denen man übrigens je nach Beschaffenheit der Stelle wechseln sollte, kommt es am Anfang nicht darauf an, sofort alle Töne und Harmonien verfolgen zu können. Viel wichtiger ist es, Bewegungsabläufe zu erkennen und nachzuvollziehen. Alles Weitere kommt mit der Erfahrung.

Verfolgen von kontrapunktischen Stimmen

Der vorliegende Ausschnitt aus Brahms' Requiem (Beispiel 6) ist polyphon komponiert, d.h. man muss mehrere gleichwertige Stimmen entweder im Wechsel (ohne den Anschluss zu verlieren) oder gleichzeitig verfolgen können.

Doch das auf den ersten Blick so übervolle Notenbild lichtet sich bald, wenn man sich die Partitur näher auf parallele Stimmen ansieht. Brahms ordnet z.B. jeder Chorstimme Orchesterstimmen zu. Das hat zur Folge, dass hier zwar viele Stimmen notiert sind, aber wesentlich weniger eigenständige Stimmen tatsächlich erklingen. Die vielen geschriebenen Noten lassen sich also auf ein überschaubares Maß reduzieren.

So werden Flöte, Klarinette, erste Violinen und Sopran parallel geführt. Des Weiteren wird der Tenor von Oboe und Bratsche mit einer stark erweiterten, aber dennoch parallel verlaufenden Stimme unterstützt. Ebenfalls fast ganz parallel verlaufen Violoncelli und Fagotte.

Zu den polyphon gefügten Stimmen erklingen die tiefen Bläser und Streicher sowie die Pauke mit Füllstimmen, welche lediglich aus Liegetönen (ausgehaltene Töne) bestehen. Sie braucht man beim ersten Lesen nicht weiter zu verfolgen.

Im Ganzen gesehen bietet sich in diesem Ausschnitt an, schwerpunktmäßig die Sopranstimme zu verfolgen, da sie mit zwei Instrumenten gekoppelt ist und als höchste Stimme gut herauszuhören ist. Zudem bietet der Text eine Orientierungshilfe, so dass der Wiedereinstieg von vorübergehenden Ausflügen in andere Stimmen erleichtert wird.

Bei fugierten Abschnitten kann man sich das Mitlesen auch erleichtern, indem man zunächst alle Einsätze des Themas in der Partitur sucht und sich markiert.

Beispiel 6 · aus: Ein deutsches Requiem von Brahms

Die Partitur im Überblick

A **Taktstriche** sind innerhalb der Instrumentengruppen durchgezogen.

B Die **Taktzahlen** erleichtern die Orientierung in der Partitur. Manchmal dienen hierzu auch Großbuchstaben, sog. Studierbuchstaben.

C Eine einzelne Zeile der Partitur nennt man **Notensystem**. Für welche(s) Instrument(e) sie steht, zeigt der **Instrumentenvorsatz** an (hier Fl. für Flöte).

D Der **Kopfstrich** verbindet alle Notensysteme miteinander zu einer **Akkolade**.

E Zusätzlich zum Kopfstrich fassen **gerade Klammern** die einzelnen Instrumentengruppen (Holz-, Blech- und Streichinstrumente) zusammen. Innerhalb dieser Gruppen sind die Instrumente nach Tonlage geordnet, wobei das höchste an oberster Stelle steht.
Die heute übliche Partituranordnung lautet von oben nach unten:
· Holzblasinstrumente
· Blechblasinstrumente
· Schlaginstrumente
· Harfe, Klavier, Celesta
· Soloinstrument(e)
· Solostimmen
· Chor
· Streichinstrumente

F Stehen zwei Akkoladen auf einer Seite, werden sie durch zwei **Schrägstriche** voneinander abgetrennt.

G Steht hinter dem Instrumentennamen z.B. „in B" oder (B), handelt es sich um ein **transponierendes Instrument**. In diesem Fall deutet das (B) an, dass das notierte C als B erklingt, also alle Noten einen Ton tiefer erklingen als sie notiert sind. Die meisten transponierenden Instrumente sind in der Partitur durch diese Zusätze leicht zu erkennen. Es gibt aber auch transponierende Instrumente ohne eine entsprechende Angabe in der Partitur, wie z.B.:
Piccoloflöte (in c/eine Oktave höher)
Englischhorn (in f/eine Quinte tiefer)
Kontrafagott (in c/eine Oktave tiefer)
Kontrabass (in c/eine Oktave tiefer)

H Die transponierenden Blechblasinstrumente haben keine Generalvorzeichen, sondern bei Bedarf Versetzungszeichen, die direkt vor der jeweiligen Note stehen.

I Die Viola oder Bratsche wird im **Alt- bzw. Bratschenschlüssel** notiert, die Stimmen des Violoncellos und Fagotts manchmal im **Tenorschlüssel**. Beide Schlüssel sind leicht zu lesen, wenn man sich klarmacht, dass der Schlüssel den Ton c1 umrahmt, also:

Alt-   Tenor-   Violinschlüssel

J Vor einem Wechsel der Ton- oder Taktart steht immer ein **Doppelstrich**. Das hier folgende Alla-Breve-Zeichen (¢) ist ebenso wie das Zeichen für den 4/4-Takt (c) ein Relikt aus einer älteren Notationspraxis und steht für den 2/2-Takt.

112

Blockweises Lesen:
Bei rhythmisch parallelgeführten Stimmen.

A

B

C

D

Selektives Lesen: Man verfolgt die führende Stimme.

E

aus: Symphonie Nr. 4 B-Dur von Beethoven

A Durch die **Tempoangabe** (manchmal mit einer Metronomzahl verbunden) gibt der Komponist an, wie schnell ein Stück gespielt werden soll.

B Bei den Bläsern werden in der Regel zwei Stimmen in einer Notenzeile zusammengefasst. Spielen sie den gleichen Ton, erhält der Notenkopf zwei Hälse oder es steht a2 darüber.

C Zweistimmige Akkorde in den Notensystemen der Streicher werden von einem Spieler gespielt. Will man die Stimmen aufteilen, schreibt man **divisi** (geteilt). Dann spielt an jedem Pult ein Spieler die oberen und ein Spieler die unteren Noten.

D Hat eine Stimme, wie hier die Flöte, längere Zeit Pause, wird ihr Notensystem oft bis zum erneuten Einsatz der Stimme weggelassen. So wird Platz gespart, man muß weniger blättern und die erklingenden Stimmen sind übersichtlicher angeordnet.

E Um Platz zu sparen und Tonfolgen übersichtlicher zu gestalten, verwendet man gelegentlich sogenannte **Abbreviaturen (Faulenzer)**. Das hier verwendete Zeichen ♩ steht für ♪♪♪♪, wobei die Halbe Note die Dauer der Wiederholungen anzeigt und der Strich durch den Notenhals den Wert der zu wiederholenden Noten (1 Strich = Achtel, 2 = Sechzehntel usw.). Vgl. auch die Viola in T. 43, in der zunächst die Repetitionen ausgeschrieben und dann abgekürzt sind.

Partiturlesen im Klassensatz

Diese kurze Einführung können Sie als kostenloses Faltblatt bestellen – gern auch im Klassensatz!

Faltblatt "Die Kunst des Partiturlesens"
Bestellnummer: ETP 9999-99 (kostenlos)

Die passende Ergänzung für Klassen- und Unterrichtsräume:

Plakat A2 "Die Partitur im Überblick"
Bestellnummer ETP 9950-99 (kostenlos)

Mozart im Klassensatz

Ein Lebens- und Reisebild
Mozart war nicht nur einer der größten Komponisten, sondern auch einer der besten Pianisten des 18. Jahrhunderts. Wie heutige Virtuosen verbrachte er große Teile seines Lebens auf Konzertreisen zwischen den führenden Höfen und großen Städten seiner Zeit. Diese kleine Broschüre entfaltet ein Panorama des europäischen Musiklebens, das den Hintergrund für Mozarts Schaffen bildete. Eine Kurzbiographie und ein kleiner Einblick in seine Schreibweise runden das Bild ab.

Faltblatt "Mozart. Ein Lebens- und Reisebild"
Bestellnummer ETP 9990-99 (kostenlos)

Weitere Informationen unter www.eulenburg.de

Eulenburg

507_01_MA 06/06